THE OFFICIAL  CHAMPIONS LEAGUE
ANNUAL 2012

Written by Pete Oliver

itv STUDIOS

The ITV Sport logo is licensed by ITV Studios Global Entertainment.
All rights reserved.

A Grange Publication

© 2011. Published by Grange Communications Ltd., Edinburgh, under licence from ITV Studios Global Entertainment. Printed in the EU.

Every effort has been made to ensure the accuracy of information within this publication but the publishers cannot be held responsible for any errors or omissions. Views expressed are those of the author and do not necessarily represent those of the publishers or ITV Studios Global Entertainment. All rights reserved.

Photographs © Action Images

ISBN 978-1-908221-21-6

£7.99

CONTENTS

Wembley Wonders	8-11
Capital Performance: The Final	12-13
Lionel Messi – The Perfect Ten	14-15
United Fall Again To Catalan Curse	16-17
The Way To Wembley	18-23
Reign Over For Ginger Prince	24-25
Champions League Quiz	27
Tottenham: Pride of London	28-29
Chelsea Still Chasing Holy Grail	30-31
Wembley: Best Of British	34-35
Gunners Silenced Again by Barca	36-37
Messi Top of the Charts	39
No Stopping Spain	41
Magic Moments	42-45
Did You Know?	47
Home Sweet Home For Walter	48-49
Champions League Wordsearch	50
Fun and Games	53
Back Home With Barca	55
Europa League: Portuguese Pride	56-59
Stat Attack	60
Quiz Answers	61

INTRODUCTION

The 2010/11 Champions League couldn't quite produce a British winner at Wembley – the home of English football.

Manchester United went close but ultimately even the class of the Premier League champions and the legendary know-how of manager Alex Ferguson couldn't find a way to halt Barcelona's march to the title.

And perhaps it was fitting that arguably one of the finest clubs sides ever, inspired by one of the best players ever in Lionel Messi, went on to lift the trophy on a dazzling night in London.

ITV Sport brought you all the action and all the drama of a vintage Champions League campaign and the Official ITV Sport Champions League Annual gives you the chance to re-live many of the highlights.

Enjoy the story of Barca's march to greatness, Tottenham's thrilling first crack at the Champions League and all the hopes and heartache that the top teams in Europe put into their tilt at glory.

Who knows who will write the script in 2011/12?

Big spending Manchester City take their place at the top table for the first time and Chelsea's exciting new coach Andre Villas-Boas will be looking to make his mark at Stamford Bridge as all roads lead to the final in Munich.

Excitement is guaranteed, and whatever happens, ITV Sport will be with you all the way.

Enjoy it with us.

WEMBLEY WONDERS

All Hail Barcelona

Brilliant Barca prove themselves the undoubted kings of Europe as they take winning the Champions League to a new level.

Barca's 3-1 demolition of Manchester United in a thrilling Champions League final at Wembley gave the Catalan conquerors a fourth European crown.

Back at the scene of their first European triumph in 1992, Barca dashed United's dreams in the final for the second time in three years.

The victory also gave the Spanish champions a third Champions League success in six years.

But it was the manner of the triumph orchestrated by Pep Guardiola's maestros that confirmed this Barcelona side as one of the greats.

Restricting United to one shot on goal, while chalking up 12 of their own and enjoying nearly 70 per cent of the possession underlined Barca's superiority over the record-breaking 19-times English champions.

And their mesmeric style of play, capped by sparkling goals from Pedro Rodriguez, Lionel Messi and David Villa lit up Wembley to make a one-sided final enthralling to watch.

"We put on a spectacle for everyone who is passionate about football and who loves football," said marauding Brazilian full-back Daniel Alves.

"And I think that people who really like football will be very happy because they have seen a great match."

WEMBLEY WONDERS

Talismanic play-maker Messi collected the individual plaudits as man of the match as he crowned another stellar performance with the second goal for Barca early in the second half.

Rodriguez had fired the Spanish giants ahead after Xavi's pass had opened up United's defence.

And even though Wayne Rooney equalised from United's best move of the night, Messi restored Barca's lead with an explosive shot which left Edwin van der Sar grasping at air on the final appearance of his illustrious career.

With Barca running riot it was no surprise when they added a third goal as Villa curled an inch-perfect shot into the top corner.

Club captain Carlos Puyol made a late appearance from the bench following injury but in an emotional finale, it was Eric Abidal who lifted the famous trophy into the London night sky less than three months after recovering from surgery to remove a cancerous tumour from his liver.

Barcelona's celebrations capped another outstanding season in which they completed their fourth double as winners of the Champions League and La Liga.

Guardiola's men brushed aside all challengers, including big rivals Real Madrid in both the Spanish league and in a bad tempered semi-final clash in Europe as Madrid manager Jose Mourinho saw his hopes of a third Champions League success with a third different club dashed in disappointing style.

In Spain, Barca shattered records left, right and centre as they racked up their 21st league title and third in a row.

And having put United to the sword in club football's showpiece event under the Wembley arch, the Catalans spelled out an emphatic claim to be considered as one of the greatest ever club sides in history.

THE FINAL

Capital Performance!

Barcelona put on a regal performance in London to win the Champions League title for a fourth time and the second time at Wembley.

Their 3-1 success prevented United from repeating their 1968 triumph at the home of English football.

Long-serving Barca captain Carlos Puyol made a late appearance as a substitute following injury.

But rather than picking up the trophy for the second time in three seasons, Puyal allowed Eric Abidal to collect the silverware – just a couple of months after the defender underwent surgery to remove a tumour on his liver.

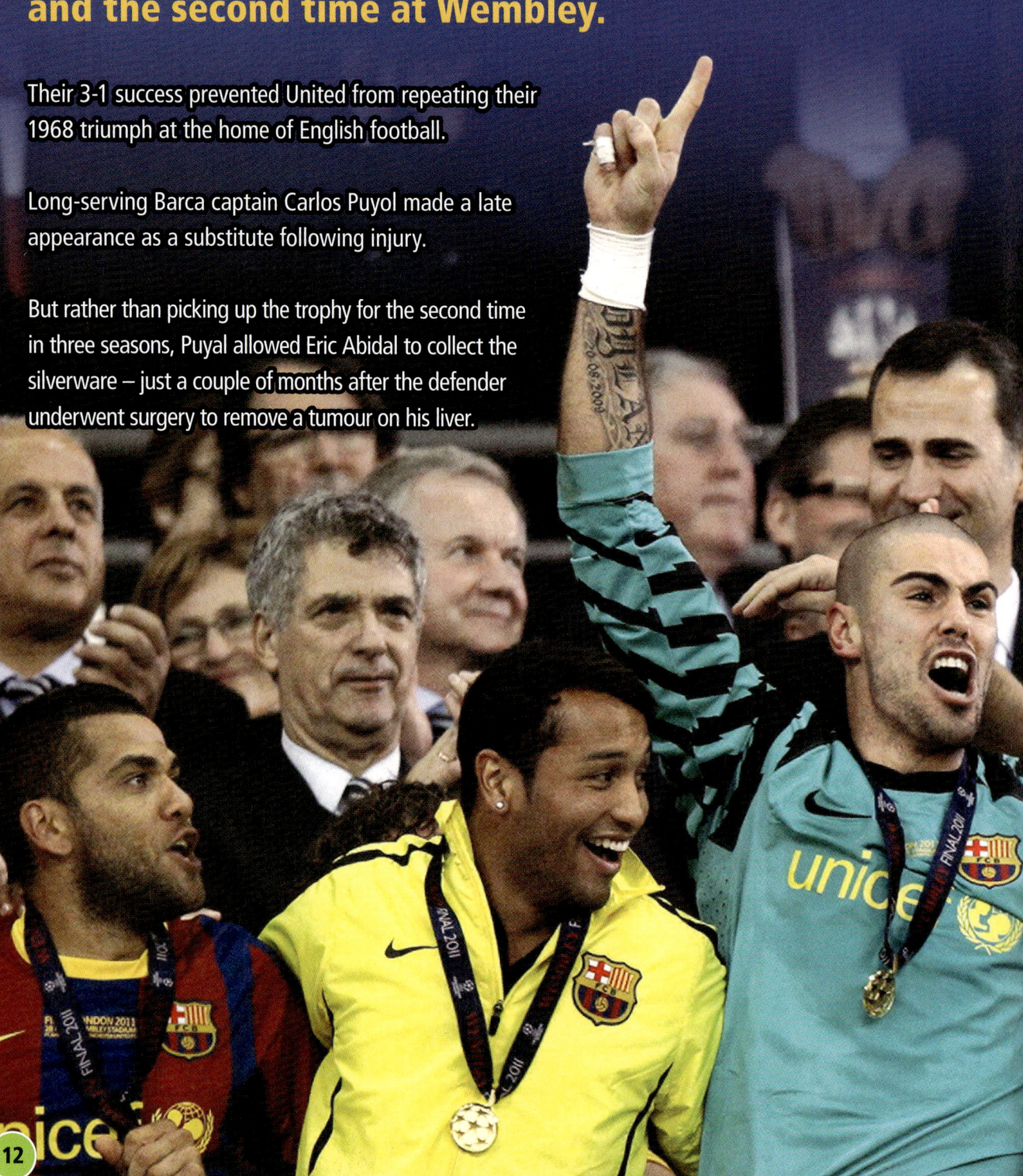

Champions League final 2011

Saturday, May 28, 2011, Wembley Stadium, London
Kick-off 7.45pm • Attendance: 87,695
Referee: V Kassai (Hungary)

Barcelona 3 (Pedrito 27, Messi 54, Villa 69)

Barcelona: Valdes, Alves (Puyol 88), Pique, Abidal, Xavi, Iniesta, Mascherano, Busquets, Villa (Keita 86), Messi, Pedrito (Afellay 90).

Substitutes not used: Olazabal, Correia, Thiago, Bojan.

Booked: Valdes, Alves.

Manchester United 1 (Rooney 34)

Manchester United: Van der Sar, Evra, Ferdinand, Vidic, Fabio Da Silva (Nani 69), Giggs, Ji-Sung, Carrick (Scholes 76), Valencia, Rooney, Hernandez.

Substitutes not used: Kuszczak, Smalling, Anderson, Fletcher, Owen.

Booked: Carrick, Valencia.

LIONEL MESSI

Messi is the Perfect Ten

Barcelona talisman Lionel Messi is on top of the world

The 'Little Magician' Lionel Messi lived up to his billing as the best player in the world as he led Barcelona to Champions League glory.

In a team of superstars it's tough to pick out one stand-out performer and Messi was quick to share the praise around his team-mates after Barca had beaten Manchester United 3-1 in the final at Wembley.

But Messi's man-of-the-match award was a fitting tribute for a player who epitomises the brilliance of Pepe Guardiola's dream team.

United manager Alex Ferguson admitted that his team couldn't control the Argentina international in a repeat of the 2009 final.

But as he added: 'Many people have said that!'

Messi restored Barca's lead with a typically thrusting run and explosive left-foot drive that gave Edwin van der Sar no chance in the United goal.

And he also mesmerised United's defence again to help create the opening for David Villa to seal Barcelona's third Champions League success in six years.

Messi's latest European master-class was the crowning glory on another outstanding year in which he became the first player to score 50 goals in a Spanish season.

Cristiano Ronaldo soon followed suit as he set a new La Liga record of 40 goals for the 2010/11 season.

The two rivals finished level in the scoring stakes with 53 apiece but when it comes to delivering the goods on the big stage, there's no-one to touch Messi.

As well as leading Barca's successful assault on the Spanish league title – his fifth – the 24-year-old was also top scorer in the Champions League for a remarkable third successive year.

Two of those came against Arsenal in the last-16 as Messi again tormented the Gunners following his four goals against the Londoners in the Nou Camp 12 months earlier.

He then scored Barca's only goal in the second leg of Barcelona's quarter-final stroll against Shakhtar Donetsk before producing one of the competition's most memorable performances in an 'El Classico' semi-final against Madrid.

An ugly game was saved by the majesty of Messi, whose second goal in a 2-0 win will go down as one of the greatest of all time as he produced a breath-taking solo run through the Madrid defence to set up a 3-1 aggregate triumph and ultimate glory at Wembley.

MANCHESTER UNITED

United Fall Again to Catalan Curse

Alex Ferguson's men are kings of England but European crown eludes them again

Manchester United were within touching distance of their own famous double before running into the might of Barcelona.

United secured a 19th English League Championship to eclipse Liverpool's record and headed to Wembley hoping for a repeat of their twin Premier League and Champions League successes of 1999 and 2008.

But even by his own admission, legendary manager Alex Ferguson admitted that Barca were just too good in the Champions League final as the Catalan kings ran out 3-1 winners.

"In my time as manager, it's the best team I've faced," admitted Ferguson.

"I think that great teams do go in cycles, and I think the cycle they're in at the moment makes them the best in Europe, there's no question of that."

Ferguson vowed to rise to the challenge of trying to topple Barca from their perch and with the Scot's phenomenal record at Old Trafford you wouldn't bet against United again emerging as the major challengers to Barcelona's grip on European football.

United had little trouble in reaching their third final in four years in 2011.

The Red Devils eased through the group stage as unbeaten Group C winners with a 100 per cent away record.

And their impressive away form also stood them in good stead in the knock-out stages as they followed up a goalless draw in Marseille with a 2-1 victory at Old Trafford to set up a mouth-watering quarter-final clash with domestic foes Chelsea.

A Wayne Rooney goal at Stamford Bridge gave United the edge and even though substitute Didier Drogba briefly made the second-leg 1-1 following Javier Hernandez's opener, ten-man Chelsea were killed off within 60 seconds when Park Ji-Sung secured his side's passage through to the last four.

Underdogs FC Schalke stood in the way of United's progress to the final and the German side put up only token resistance as goals from the ageless Ryan Giggs and the in-form Rooney in Gelsenkirchen all but booked a Wembley place.

Schalke goalkeeper Manuel Neuer produced an outstanding display to limit the damage but even he couldn't prevent a 4-1 beating in the return leg as Antonio Valencia, Darron Gibson and Anderson, twice, scored to set up a repeat of the 2009 final.

Sadly for United, the outcome was also the same.

THE WAY TO WEMBLEY

Group Stage Results 2010/11

Matchday One: 14.09.2010

Grp		Result	
D	Barcelona	5:1	Panathinaikos
B	Benfica	2:0	Hapoel Tel Aviv
C	Bursaspor	0:4	Valencia
D	FC Copenhagen	1:0	Rubin
C	Manchester United	0:0	Rangers
B	Olympique Lyonnais	1:0	Schalke 04
A	Twente	2:2	Inter
A	Werder	2:2	Tottenham Hotspur

Matchday One: 15.09.2010

Grp		Result	
H	Arsenal	6:0	Sporting Braga
E	Bayern Munich	2:0	Roma
E	CFR 1907 Cluj	2:1	Basel
G	Milan	2:0	Auxerre
F	MSK Zilina	1:4	Chelsea
F	Olympique Marseille	0:1	Spartak Moscow
G	Real	2:0	Ajax
H	Shakhtar	1:0	Partizan

Matchday Two: 28.09.2010

Grp		Result	
G	Ajax	1:1	Milan
G	Auxerre	0:1	Real
E	Basel	1:2	Bayern Munich
F	Chelsea	2:0	Olympique Marseille
H	Partizan	1:3	Arsenal
E	Roma	2:1	CFR 1907 Cluj
F	Spartak Moscow	3:0	MSK Zilina
H	Sporting Braga	0:3	Shakhtar

Matchday Two: 29.09.2010

Grp		Result	
B	Hapoel Tel Aviv	1:3	Olympique Lyonnais
A	Inter	4:0	Werder
D	Panathinaikos	0:2	FC Copenhagen
C	Rangers	1:0	Bursaspor
D	Rubin	1:1	Barcelona
B	Schalke 04	2:0	Benfica
A	Tottenham Hotspur	4:1	Twente
C	Valencia	0:1	Manchester United

Matchday Three: 19.10.2010

Grp		Result	
G	Ajax	2:1	Auxerre
H	Arsenal	5:1	Shakhtar
E	Bayern Munich	3:2	CFR 1907 Cluj
F	Olympique Marseille	1:0	MSK Zilina
G	Real	2:0	Milan
E	Roma	1:3	Basel
F	Spartak Moscow	0:2	Chelsea
H	Sporting Braga	2:0	Partizan

Matchday Three: 20.10.2010

Grp		Result	
D	Barcelona	2:0	FC Kobenhavn
A	Inter	4:3	Tottenham Hotspur
C	Manchester United	1:0	Bursaspor
B	Olympique Lyonnais	2:0	Benfica
D	Panathinaikos	0:0	Rubin
C	Rangers	1:1	Valencia
B	Schalke 04	3:1	Hapoel Tel Aviv
A	Twente	1:1	Werder

Matchday Four: 02.11.2010

Grp		Result	
B	Benfica	4:3	Olympique Lyonnais
C	Bursaspor	0:3	Manchester United
D	FC Copenhagen	1:1	Barcelona
B	Hapoel Tel Aviv	0:0	Schalke 04
D	Rubin	0:0	Panathinaikos
A	Tottenham Hotspur	3:1	Inter
C	Valencia	3:0	Rangers
A	Werder	0:2	Twente

Matchday Four: 03.11.2010

Grp		Result	
G	Auxerre	2:1	Ajax
E	Basel	2:3	Roma
E	CFR 1907 Cluj	0:4	Bayern Munich
F	Chelsea	4:1	Spartak Moskva
G	Milan	2:2	Real
F	MSK Zilina	0:7	Olympique Marseille
H	Partizan	0:1	Sporting Braga
H	Shakhtar	2:1	Arsenal

Matchday Five: 23.11.2010

Grp		Result	
G	Ajax	0:4	Real
G	Auxerre	0:2	Milan
E	Basel	1:0	CFR 1907 Cluj
F	Chelsea	2:1	MSK Zilina
H	Partizan	0:3	Shakhtar
E	Roma	3:2	Bayern Munich
F	Spartak Moscow	0:3	Olympique Marseille
H	Sporting Braga	2:0	Arsenal

Matchday Five: 24.11.2010

Grp		Result	
B	Hapoel Tel Aviv	3:0	Benfica
A	Inter	1:0	Twente
D	Panathinaikos	0:3	Barcelona
C	Rangers	0:1	Manchester United
D	Rubin	1:0	FC Copenhagen
B	Schalke 04	3:0	Olympique Lyonnais
A	Tottenham Hotspur	3:0	Werder
C	Valencia	6:1	Bursaspor

Matchday Six: 07.12.2010

Grp		Result	
D	Barcelona	2:0	Rubin
B	Benfica	1:2	Schalke 04
C	Bursaspor	1:1	Rangers
D	FC Copenhagen	3:1	Panathinaikos
C	Manchester United	1:1	Valencia
B	Olympique Lyonnais	2:2	Hapoel Tel Aviv
A	Twente	3:3	Tottenham Hotspur
A	Werder	3:0	Inter

Matchday Six: 08.12.2010

Grp		Result	
H	Arsenal	3:1	Partizan
E	Bayern Munich	3:0	Basel
E	CFR 1907 Cluj	1:1	Roma
G	Milan	0:2	Ajax
F	MSK Zilina	1:2	Spartak Moscow
F	Olympique Marseille	1:0	Chelsea
G	Real	4:0	Auxerre
H	Shakhtar	2:0	Sporting Braga

THE WAY TO WEMBLEY

Group Tables 2010/11

Group A

TEAM	P	W	D	L	F	A	GD	PTS
Tottenham Hotspur	6	3	2	1	18	11	+7	11
Internazionale	6	3	1	2	12	11	+11	10
Twente	6	1	3	2	9	11	-2	6
Werder Bremen	6	1	2	3	6	12	-6	5

Group B

TEAM	P	W	D	L	F	A	GD	PTS
Schalke 04	6	4	1	1	10	3	+7	13
Lyon	6	3	1	2	11	10	+1	10
Benfica	6	2	0	4	7	12	-5	6
Hapoel Tel Aviv	6	1	2	3	7	10	-3	5

Group C

TEAM	P	W	D	L	F	A	GD	PTS
Manchester United	6	4	2	0	7	1	+6	14
Valencia	6	3	2	1	15	4	+11	11
Rangers	6	1	3	2	3	6	-3	6
Bursaspor	6	0	1	5	2	16	-14	1

Group D

TEAM	P	W	D	L	F	A	GD	PTS
Barcelona	6	4	2	0	14	3	+11	14
Copenhagen	6	3	1	2	7	5	+2	10
Rubin Kazan	6	1	3	2	2	4	-2	6
Panathinaikos	6	0	2	4	2	13	-11	2

Group E

TEAM	P	W	D	L	F	A	GD	PTS
Bayern Munich	6	5	0	1	16	6	+10	15
Roma	6	3	1	2	10	11	-1	10
Basel	6	2	0	4	8	11	-3	6
CFR Cluj	6	1	1	4	6	12	-6	4

Group F

TEAM	P	W	D	L	F	A	GD	PTS
Chelsea	6	5	0	1	14	4	+10	15
Marseille	6	4	0	2	12	3	+9	12
Spartak Moscow	6	3	0	3	7	10	-3	9
Žilina	6	0	0	6	3	19	-16	0

Group G

TEAM	P	W	D	L	F	A	GD	PTS
Real Madrid	6	5	1	0	15	2	+13	16
Milan	6	2	2	2	7	7	0	8
Ajax	6	2	1	3	6	10	-4	7
Auxerre	6	1	0	5	3	12	-9	3

Group H

TEAM	P	W	D	L	F	A	GD	PTS
Shakhtar Donetsk	6	5	0	1	12	6	+6	15
Arsenal	6	4	0	2	18	7	+11	12
Braga	6	3	0	3	5	11	-6	9
Partizan	6	0	0	6	2	13	-11	0

THE WAY TO WEMBLEY

FIRST KNOCK-OUT ROUND

🇫🇷 Lyon	1	0	1
🇪🇸 Real Madrid	1	3	4

🇮🇹 Milan	0	0	0
🏴󠁧󠁢󠁥󠁮󠁧󠁿 Tottenham Hotspur	1	0	1

🏴󠁧󠁢󠁥󠁮󠁧󠁿 Arsenal	2	1	3
🇪🇸 Barcelona	1	3	4

🇮🇹 Roma	2	0	2
🇺🇦 Shakhtar Donetsk	3	3	6

🇮🇹 Internazionale (a)	0	3	3
🇩🇪 Bayern Munich	1	2	3

🇪🇸 Valencia	1	1	2
🇩🇪 Schalke 04	1	3	4

🇩🇰 Copenhagen	0	0	0
🏴󠁧󠁢󠁥󠁮󠁧󠁿 Chelsea	2	0	2

🇫🇷 Marseille	0	1	1
🏴󠁧󠁢󠁥󠁮󠁧󠁿 Manchester United	0	2	2

QUARTER-FINALS

🇪🇸 Real Madrid	4	1	5
🏴󠁧󠁢󠁥󠁮󠁧󠁿 Tottenham Hotspur	0	0	0

🇪🇸 Barcelona	5	1	6
🇺🇦 Shakhtar Donetsk	1	0	1

🇮🇹 Internazionale (a)	2	1	3
🇩🇪 Schalke 04	5	2	7

🏴󠁧󠁢󠁥󠁮󠁧󠁿 Chelsea	0	1	1
🏴󠁧󠁢󠁥󠁮󠁧󠁿 Manchester United	1	2	3

SEMI-FINALS

FINAL

| 🇪🇸 Barcelona | | | 3 |
| 🏴󠁧󠁢󠁥󠁮󠁧󠁿 Manchester United | | | 1 |

| 🇪🇸 Real Madrid | 0 | 1 | **1** |
| 🇪🇸 **Barcelona** | 2 | 1 | **3** |

| 🇩🇪 Schalke 04 | 0 | 1 | **1** |
| 🏴󠁧󠁢󠁥󠁮󠁧󠁿 **Manchester United** | 2 | 4 | **6** |

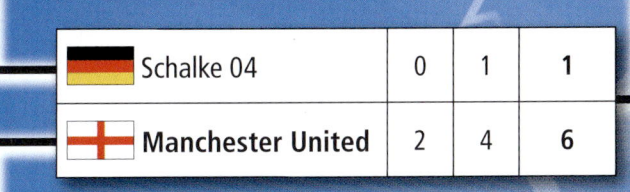

23

PAUL SCHOLES

Glorious Reign Over for the Ginger Prince

Final defeat can't tarnish the career of Old Trafford legend Paul Scholes

The 2011 Champions League final signalled the end of one of the greatest careers in English football history.

There was to be no fairytale end for Manchester United midfielder Paul Scholes as he collected only a losers' medal at Wembley.

But the 'Ginger Prince' could still claim to have bowed out at the top after helping United win a record 19th English league title.

Scholes made 676 appearances for United – his only club – after making his debut in 1994.

He helped United win ten domestic titles, three FA Cups, two League Cups and the Champions League in 2008.

Cruelly suspension ruled Scholes out of the 1999 Champions League final when United beat Bayern Munich.

But the Salford-born schemer, who was 36 when he retired at the end of the 2010/11 season, could rightly claim to be one of the finest players of his generation and one of United's greatest ever servants, with only three players making more appearances for the Old Trafford giants.

"I am not a man of many words but I can honestly say that playing football is all I have ever wanted to do and to have had such a long and successful career at Manchester United has been a real honour," he said after hanging up his boots.

Scholes, who scored 102 Premier League goals and won 66 England caps, was hailed as a truly unbelievable player by manager Alex Ferguson.

And the former United junior, who came through the club's youth ranks with David Beckham, Ryan Giggs, Nicky Butt, Keith Gillespie and Gary and Phil Neville, will now try and pass on some of that magic to the next crop of young stars as a coach at Old Trafford.

QUIZ

Champions League Quiz

Test your Champions League knowledge in this fun quiz.

 1. Who scored the first goal for Barcelona in the 2011 Champions League final?

 2. Which country does 2011 final referee Viktor Kassai come from?

 3. Which club knocked Chelsea out of the 2010/11 Champions League?

 4. Who scored a hat-trick against the defending champions for Tottenham in the group stages of the 2010/11 Champions League?

 5. Which club became the first team from Denmark to reach the knock-out stages of the Champions League in 2010/11?

 6. Which country do Rubin Kazan play in?

 7. Who is the all-time leading scorer in the Champions League?

 8. Which club has signed goalkeeper Manuel Neuer from FC Shalke?

 9. As well as Paul Scholes, which other Manchester United player retired after the 2011 Champions League final?

 10. Which player, rather than the captain, collected the Champions League trophy for Barcelona at Wembley?

 11. Where will the 2012 Champions League final be played?

 12. Which English team has qualified for the Champions League for the first time in 2011/12.

Answers on page 61

TOTTENHAM

Spurs are Pride of London

Cockerill crows down the Lane as Tottenham live the Champions League dream

Tottenham breathed a welcome blast of fresh air into the 2010/11 Champions League from an English point of view as they broke the Premier League's big four stranglehold on the competition.

But Harry Redknapp's entertainers had to do it the hard way after nearly falling at the first hurdle and seeing all their hard work go to waste.

Having earned a crack at the premier European competition for the first time in almost half a century, Spurs started in the final qualifying round.

And after half an hour of their first game, they were 3-0 down to Swiss club Young Boys!

Away goals from Sebastien Bassong and Roman Pavlyuchenko eased the pressure and a comfortable 4-0 win at White Hart Lane booked Tottenham's place in the group phase.

And that goal spree set the tone as Tottenham went on to finish as top scorers in the group stage as surprise winners of Group A.

Among the highlights were a thrilling comeback at Internazionale where Gareth Bale's stunning hat-trick had the defending champions hanging onto a 4-3 win.

And a 100 per cent home record, including another Bale-inspired 3-1 win over Inter, sent the Londoners marching on.

The last-16 draw gave Redknapp's men another daunting test against seven-times European champions AC Milan but once again they defied the odds to secure a famous win.

Some fine saves from Heurelho Gomes kept Milan at bay and then with ten minutes to go, Aaron Lennon broke away and crossed for Peter Crouch to slot home a famous winner.

With a precious away goal under their belts, Spurs then threw up the barricades back in London to secure a shut-out and a memorable victory as Redknapp became the first English manager to take a side into the last eight of the Champions League.

Waiting in the quarter-finals was Jose Mourinho and his Real Madrid side and the Spanish giants finally proved one obstacle too many for Tottenham to overcome.

After going behind to an early goal from ex-Arsenal man Emmanuel Adebayor, Crouch's dismissal left Tottenham up against it and shipping three more goals all but spelled their exit from the competition.

Madrid duly wrapped up victory with a 1-0 success in the second leg, but White Hart Lane rightly acclaimed their Champions League heroes as Spurs bowed out as the most gallant of losers.

"The Champions League has been great for us," said a proud Redknapp.

"We've seen some fantastic football here at White Hart Lane and away from home.

"To have come as far as we have in our first season in the Champions League and to play the way we have has been great for everybody. It's been a great experience for me and the players."

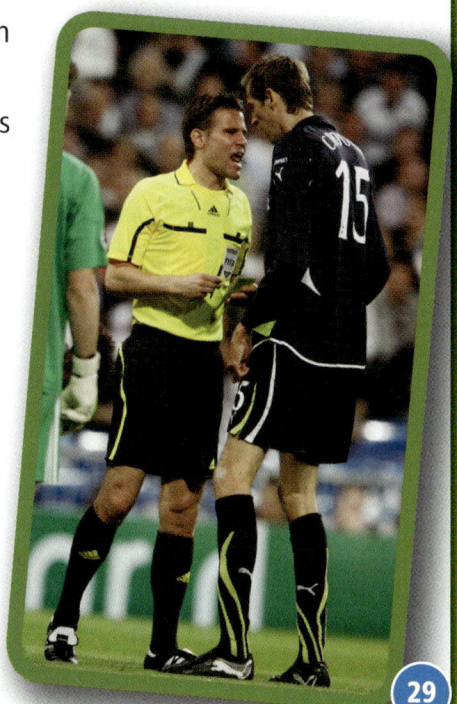

CHELSEA

Chelsea Still Chasing the Holy Grail

End of the road for Ancelotti as Blues turn to Villas-Boas

Chelsea's frustrating wait to win the Champions League goes on after their tilt at the trophy in 2010/11 ended in disappointment.

And with the ultimate prize again eluding the big-spending Londoners, manager Carlo Ancelotti paid the price with his job.

Despite leading Chelsea to a domestic double in 2010, there was to be no attempt at third time lucky in Europe for the Italian as the Blues turned to rising star Andre Villas-Boas to try and lead them to the 'Holy Grail' of the Champions League title.

Ancelotti won the European Cup as a player and a manager with AC Milan but couldn't repeat the magic at Stamford Bridge, paving the way for owner Roman Ambramovich to swoop for Portuguese prospect Villas-Boas.

"He has already achieved much in a relatively short space of time. His ambition, drive and determination matches that of Chelsea and we are confident Andre's leadership of the team will result in greater successes in major domestic and European competitions," trumpeted Chelsea.

After showing the Midas touch to the start of his managerial career with FC Porto, the former Chelsea coach, who previously spent three years in the Blues' backroom staff, returned to occupy the hot-seat once famously filled by mentor Jose Mourinho.

Appointed on a three-year contract at the age of only 33, Villas-Boas has big boots to fill.

But he was confident of being able to meet the challenge before kicking off his first season at the helm.

"I think there is no way you can avoid comparison, it is something that is the interest of the media. (But) I didn't take the Porto job, nor the Chelsea job, because Jose made the same steps," Villas-Boas told Chelsea TV.

"They are two of the most sought-after clubs in the world and in the end I had the opportunity

and was able to make them find something in me that they thought would continue their route to success.

"Chelsea is a club that in the last six years has achieved so much and people are expecting us to be the same way.

"I feel confident I can respond to the ambitions of the supporters and the ambitions of the owner and the administration."

Chelsea will hope Villas-Boas can go even closer than their near-miss of 2008, when only a penalty shoot-out defeat to Manchester United in the final in Moscow prevented Chelsea from winning the Champions League.

And it was United who ended the Blues' latest attempt as they won their quarter-final clash before also pipping them to the Premier League title in 2011.

Ancelotti's side had cantered through the group phase of their European campaign with their only defeat coming in the final game against Marseilles when both sides had already qualified.

But the cracks were perhaps beginning to show as that defeat in France came as part of a run in which Chelsea won only once in eight games.

However, the mid-winter break from European competition did help the Blues regain some momentum - despite losing their grip on the FA Cup - and when they resumed their Champions League bid in the last-16 round they comfortably eased past FC Copenhagen.

January signing Fernando Torres was still waiting for his first goal for his new club but two from strike partner Nicolas Anelka secured a 2-0 win in Denmark.

A goalless return leg secured Chelsea's passage into the last eight but probably not the draw they wanted as they were paired with United.

And an away goal from Wayne Rooney gave the Red Devils an advantage they wouldn't relinquish as they marched on towards the final via a fourth semi in five years.

Didier Drogba rose off the bench to give Chelsea brief hope as he made the second leg 1-1 but Park Ji-Sung's rapid response condemned Ancelotti's men to a 3-1 aggregate defeat and effectively signalled another new chapter of the Stamford Bridge story.

WEMBLEY

Best of British

Wembley puts on a show as the Champions League books in again for 2013.

Wembley provided a fantastic setting for the 2011 final where Barcelona did the surroundings justice by turning on the style to beat Manchester United 3-1.

And the success of the venue and the upcoming 150th anniversary of the Football Association means that the Champions League final will be returning to the home of English football in 2013.

The 2012 final will be held in the Allianz Arena in Germany – the home of Bayern Munich and TSV 1860 Munich.

And 12 months later it will be back in London with Wembley getting the nod from UEFA's Executive Committee to stage the showpiece final for a sixth time.

The first was in 1963 when AC Milan beat Benfica 2-1 in front of a crowd of 45,700.

Others winners under what were the famous Twin Towers were Manchester United (1968), Ajax (1971), Liverpool (1978) and Barcelona (1992).

The former Wembley stadium was then demolished in 2003 and its replacement built on the same site at a cost of around £800 million.

It was opened in 2007 and as well as the hosting all of England's domestic cup finals will also be the venue for the football finals at the 2012 Olympics.

Built with a sliding roof, the stand-out feature of the 'new' Wembley is the magnificent 300-metre arch which loops majestically over the stadium and will light up again for the cream of Europe in 2013.

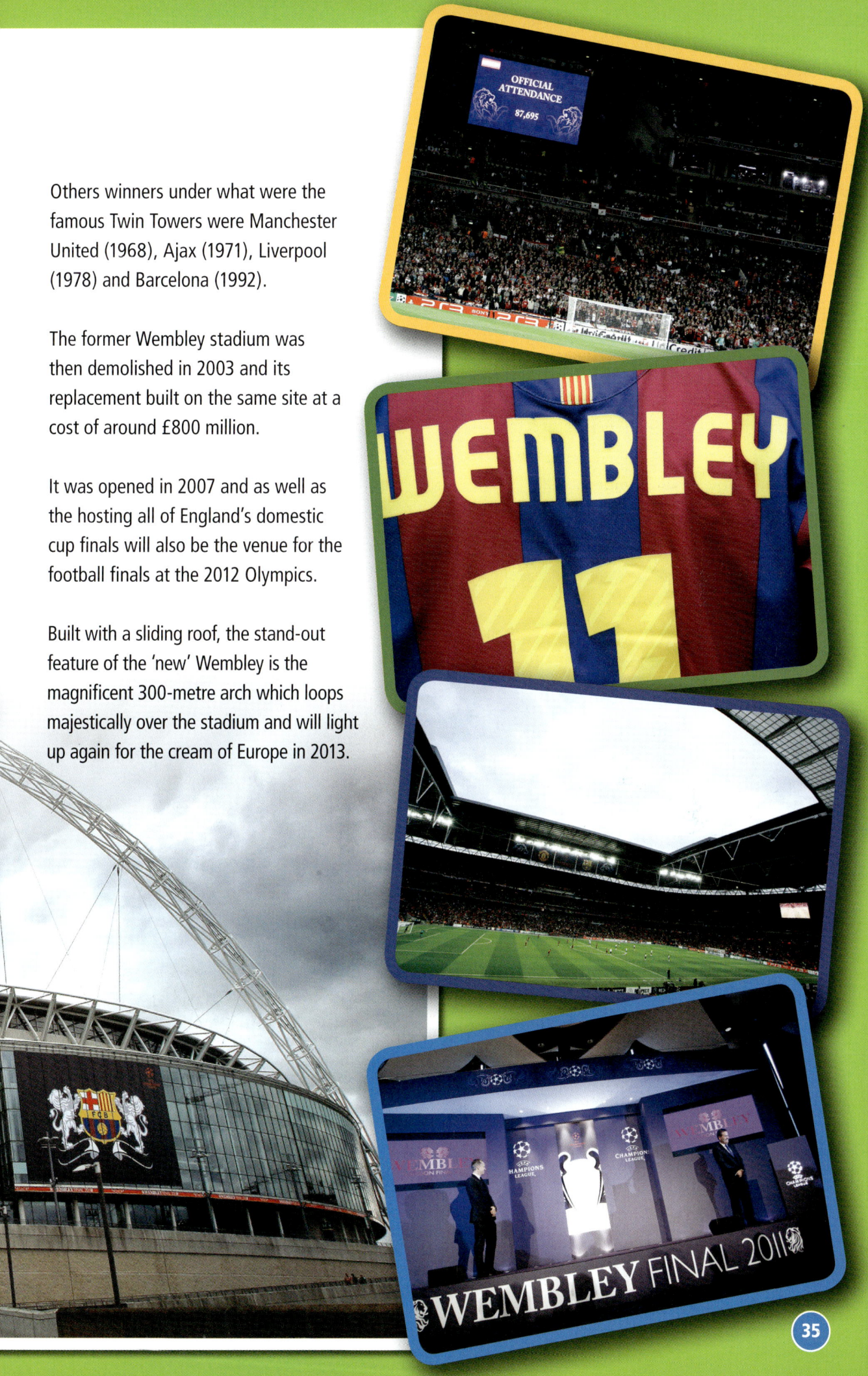

ARSENAL

Gunners Silenced Again by Mighty Barca

Arsenal maintain proud record of knock-out qualification but no nearer Euro glory

Manchester United weren't the only ones to find Barcelona blocking their path to European glory as Arsenal again saw their hopes of a first Champions League success dashed by the kings of Catalonia.

It was the Gunners' misfortune to be paired with Barca in the last 16 of the tournament after losing to Pepe Guardiola's side at the quarter-final stage in 2010.

Arsenal did at least gain the consolation of a first-ever win over Barca but even that wasn't enough to stop the ultimate winners in their tracks.

Arsene Wenger's men won the first leg of their knock-out clash at the Emirates Stadium as they came from behind to secure a dramatic 2-1 victory.

David Villa gave Barca the lead and for once Lionel Messi didn't have his shooting boots on as the Spanish champions couldn't add to their lead.

And in a fabulous fightback, Arsenal levelled through Robin van Persie's clever near-post finish before Andrey Arshavin came off the bench to grab a dramatic winner.

"It was one of those special nights and we needed to be a special team. The game promised a lot and it didn't disappoint. It was a game between two special teams in my opinion," said Wenger.

Unfortunately for the Arsenal boss that was as good as it got, though, as Barca, inspired by Messi, reversed the outcome in the Nou Camp with a 4-3 aggregate success taking them through to the quarter-finals.

It wasn't all plain-sailing as Sergio Busquets' own-goal cancelled out Messi's stunning opener and substitute goalkeeper Manuel Almunia repelled anything Barca could throw at him.

But van Persie's dismissal and Barca's pressure finally took its toll as Xavi and Messi, from the penalty spot, finally silenced the Gunners.

It had also been a roller-coaster ride for Arsenal during the group stage as despite an early goal-fest – with Braga and Shakhtar Donetsk conceding a combined total of 11 goals in two games at the Emirates – it needed a 3-1 home win in their last game against Partizan Belgrade to take the Londoners through.

An 11th successive qualification for the knock-out stages represented some achievement but still took Arsenal no nearer to winning the top prize in European football.

TOP OF THE CHARTS

Messi Top of the Charts Again

Barcelona hot shot is leading scorer for third year in a row

Lionel Messi's status as the top marksman in Europe is beyond question as he finished leading scorer yet again in the 2010/11 Champions League.

Messi's goal in the final took his tally for the campaign to 12 – four clear of his nearest challengers.

His Wembley strike not only helped Barca win the trophy but also equalled the previous record for a Champions League season set by Manchester United's Ruud van Nistelrooy in 2003.

Messi also moved level with the Dutch striker as the highest scorer in a season three times since the Champions League format was introduced in 1993.

CHAMPIONS LEAGUE TOP SCORERS 2010/11	
12	Lionel Messi (FC Barcelona)
8	Samuel Eto'o (FC Internazionale Milano), Mario Gomez (FC Bayern München)
7	Nicolas Anelka (Chelsea FC)
6	Karim Benzema, Cristiano Ronaldo (both Real Madrid CF), Roberto Soldado (Valencia CF)
5	Raúl González (FC Schalke 04)

CHAMPIONS LEAGUE TOP SCORERS BY SEASON		
1993/94	8	Ronald Koeman (FC Barcelona), Wynton Rufer (SV Werder Bremen)
1994/95	7	George Weah (Paris Saint-Germain FC)
1995/96	9	Jari Litmanen (AFC Ajax)
1996/97	5	Milinko Pantić (Club Atlético de Madrid)
1997/98	10	Alessandro Del Piero (Juventus)
1998/99	8	Andriy Shevchenko (FC Dynamo Kyiv), Dwight Yorke (Manchester United FC)
1999/00	10	Mário Jardel (FC Porto), Rivaldo (FC Barcelona), Raúl González (Real Madrid CF)
2000/01	7	Raúl González (Real Madrid CF)
2001/02	10	Ruud van Nistelrooy (Manchester United FC)
2002/03	12	Ruud van Nistelrooy (Manchester United FC)
2003/04	9	Fernando Morientes (AS Monaco FC)
2004/05	8	Ruud van Nistelrooy (Manchester United FC)
2005/06	9	Andriy Shevchenko (AC Milan)
2006/07	10	Kaká (AC Milan)
2007/08	8	Cristiano Ronaldo (Manchester United FC)
2008/09	9	Lionel Messi (FC Barcelona)
2009/10	8	Lionel Messi (FC Barcelona)
2010/11	12	Lionel Messi (FC Barcelona)

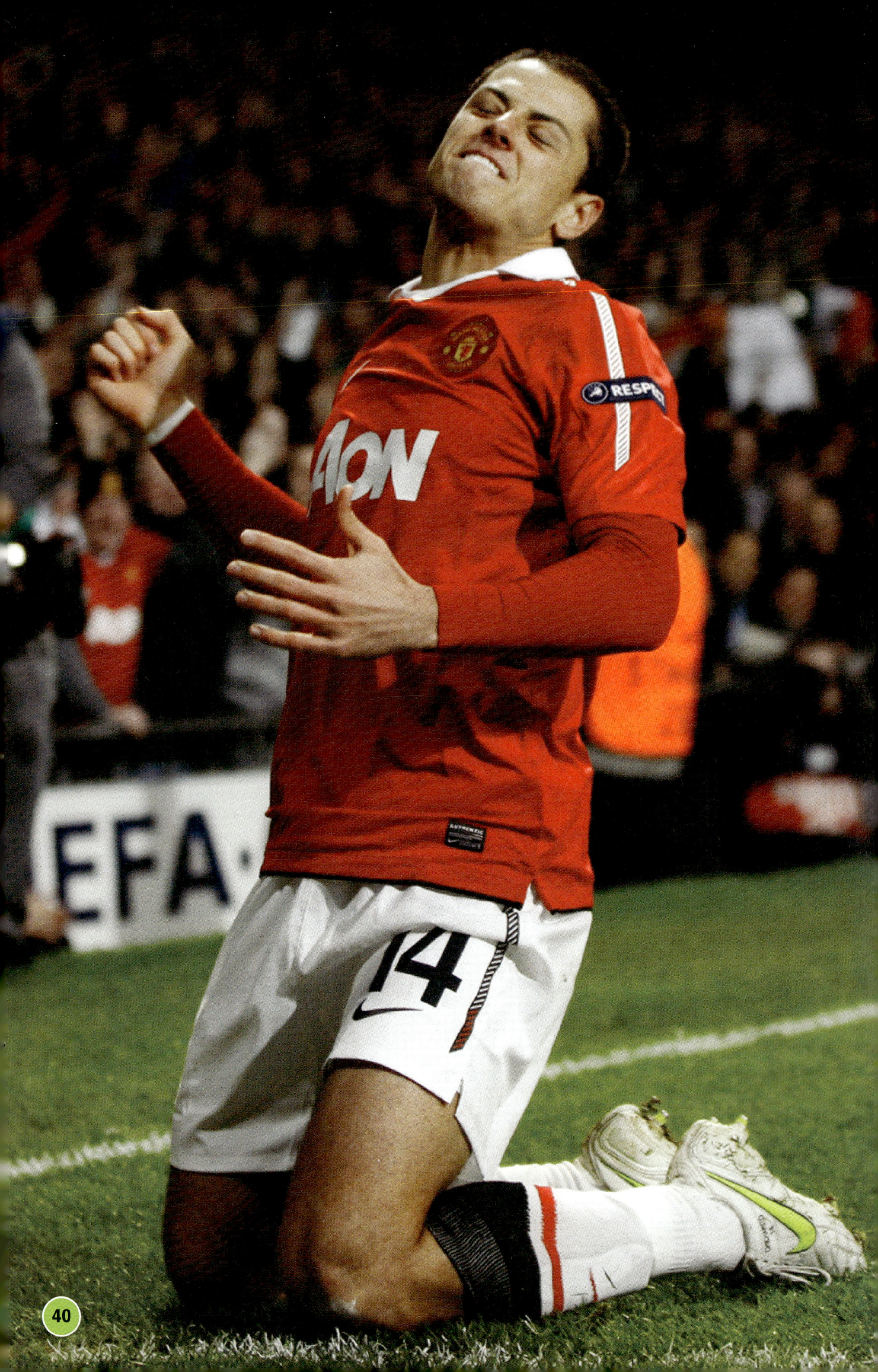
AON
14

NO STOPPING SPAIN

Barca Victory Takes Spain to the Top of the Champions' list

Spain's current domination of world football was reinforced by Barcelona's triumph in the 2010/11 Champions League final.

As a nation, Spain are reigning World Cup holders and European Champions.

And Barca's victory in the Champions League also restored Spain to the top of the winners' list in Europe's elite club competition.

Inter Milan had levelled it up for Italy in 2010 but Barcelona's fourth victory in the competition – and third in five years – restored Spain to the top of the pile.

EUROPEAN CUP/CHAMPIONS LEAGUE WINNERS BY COUNTRY

13	Spain
12	Italy
11	England
6	Germany, Netherlands
4	Portugal
1	France, Romania, Scotland, Serbia

EUROPEAN CUP/CHAMPIONS LEAGUE WINNERS

9	Real Madrid CF (ESP)
7	AC Milan (ITA)
5	Liverpool FC (ENG)
4	AFC Ajax (NED), FC Bayern München (GER), FC Barcelona (ESP)
3	FC Internazionale Milano (ITA), Manchester United FC (ENG)
2	SL Benfica (POR), Juventus (ITA), Nottingham Forest FC (ENG), FC Porto (POR)
1	Celtic FC (SCO), Hamburger SV (GER), FC Steaua Bucuresti (ROU), Olympique de Marseille (FRA), Feyenoord (NED), Aston Villa FC (ENG), PSV Eindhoven (NED), FK Crvena zvezda (SRB), Borussia Dortmund (GER)

MAGIC MOMENTS

The Champions League of 2010/11 was another vintage season in the competition's illustrious history as the cream once again rose to the top. Here we pick our ten magic moments of a golden year.

1 It wouldn't be a top ten without a couple of entries for Lionel Messi.

The first is his goal against Arsenal in the Nou Camp, a magnificent finish when he flicked the ball over Gunners' keeper Manuel Almunia before volleying home to help Barca into the quarter-finals.

2 Gareth Bale was arguably the player of the group stages as the Welsh wizard inspired Tottenham's run to the quarter-finals.

Even though it came in a losing cause, no one will forget Bale's scintillating hat-trick against Inter Milan in the San Siro.

3 When Raul left Real Madrid it looked as though the legendary striker might be winding down his career.

But a magical first season at FC Schalke saw Raul help the German club reach the semi-finals of the Champions League for the first time.

His five goals in the competition, including two in the quarter-finals against holders Inter, extended his record tally in the Champions League to 71.

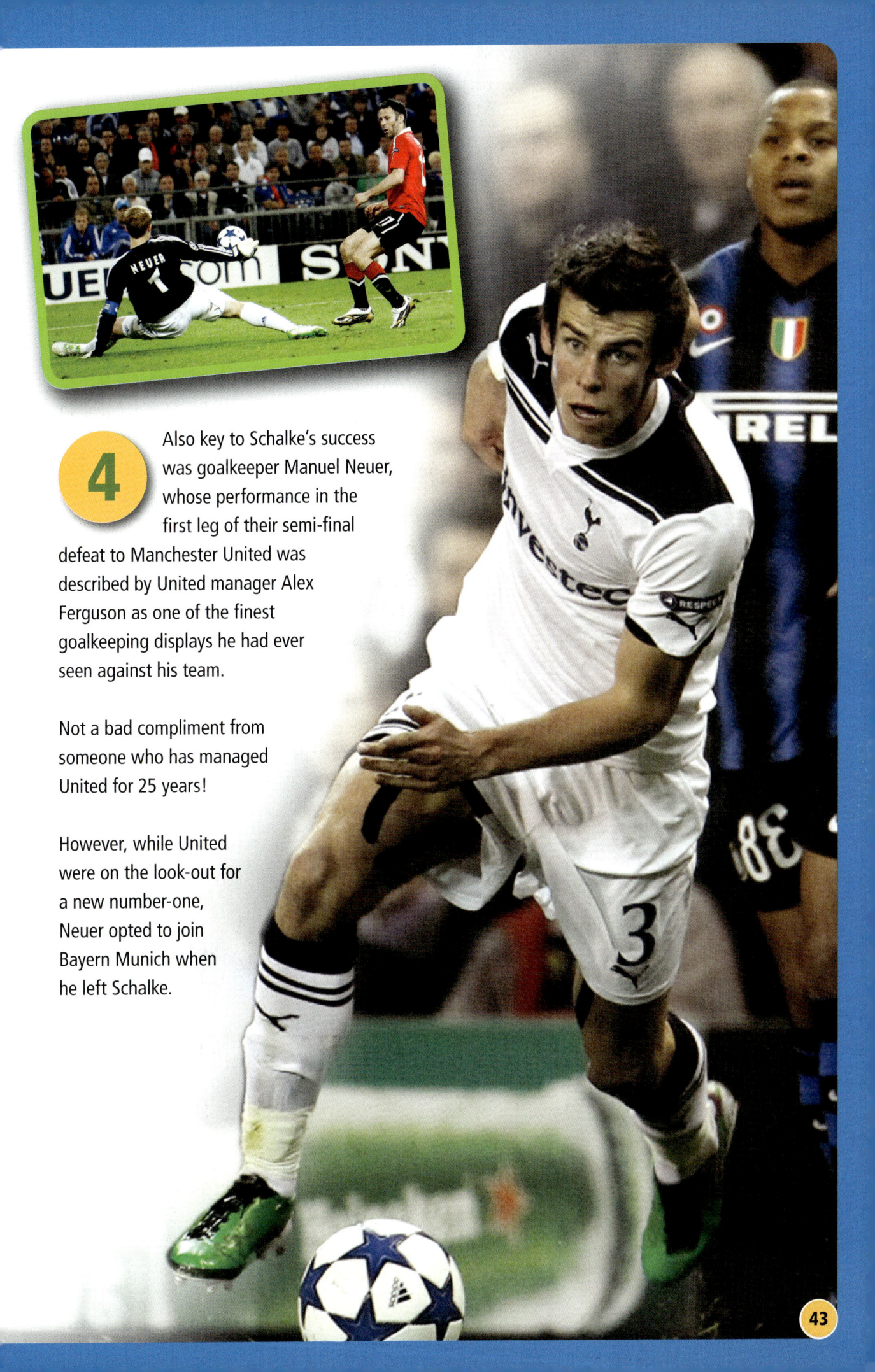

4 Also key to Schalke's success was goalkeeper Manuel Neuer, whose performance in the first leg of their semi-final defeat to Manchester United was described by United manager Alex Ferguson as one of the finest goalkeeping displays he had ever seen against his team.

Not a bad compliment from someone who has managed United for 25 years!

However, while United were on the look-out for a new number-one, Neuer opted to join Bayern Munich when he left Schalke.

MAGIC MOMENTS

5 Jose Mourinho is not everyone's cup of tea and the Real Madrid manager was hit with an initial five-match ban by UEFA for his conduct in Real's ill-tempered semi-final defeat against Barcelona.

But the Portuguese, twice a Champions League winner with Porto and Inter Milan, again proved his pedigree by taking Madrid to the last four for the first time since 2003.

And but for the controversial dismissal of Pepe in the first leg of the semi-final against Barca, Mourinho might have found a way to stop the champions. Not pretty but it might have been effective.

6 Inter Milan were unable to maintain their grip on the Champions League trophy but had the small consolation of scoring arguably the goal of the goal of the tournament thanks to Dejan Stankovic's stunning strike against Schalke.

The Serbian international collected a headed clearance from goalkeeper Manuel Neuer and let fly with a first-time volley from just inside the Schalke half which flew into the unguarded net.

7 Pushing it close was Israeli international Eran Zahavi's flying bicycle kick for Hapoel Tel-Aviv against Olympique Lyonnais in their Group B encounter.

8 Time for another Lionel Messi entry and his goal against arch rivals Real Madrid in the semi-finals.

The 'El Classico' had been an ugly scrap until Messi broke the deadlock with a neat near-post finish. But that was nothing on his second goal as the Barcelona talisman weaved his way through the bamboozled Madrid defence to effectively book Barca's place in the final.

9 Manchester United unearthed a new star in 2010/11 in the shape of striker Javier Hernandez.

The 'Little Pea' enjoyed an outstanding first season at Old Trafford, scoring 20 goals.

Four of those came in the Champions League, including three in the knock-out stages to help United reach the final.

And the emergence of the 23-year-old meant Alex Ferguson couldn't even find a place in his matchday squad at Wembley for top Premier League scorer Dimitar Berbatov.

10 Only one place to finish – Barcelona's complete mastery of Manchester United and anything else the best of Europe could throw at them as they were deservedly crowned Champions League winners. Has there been a better team?

45

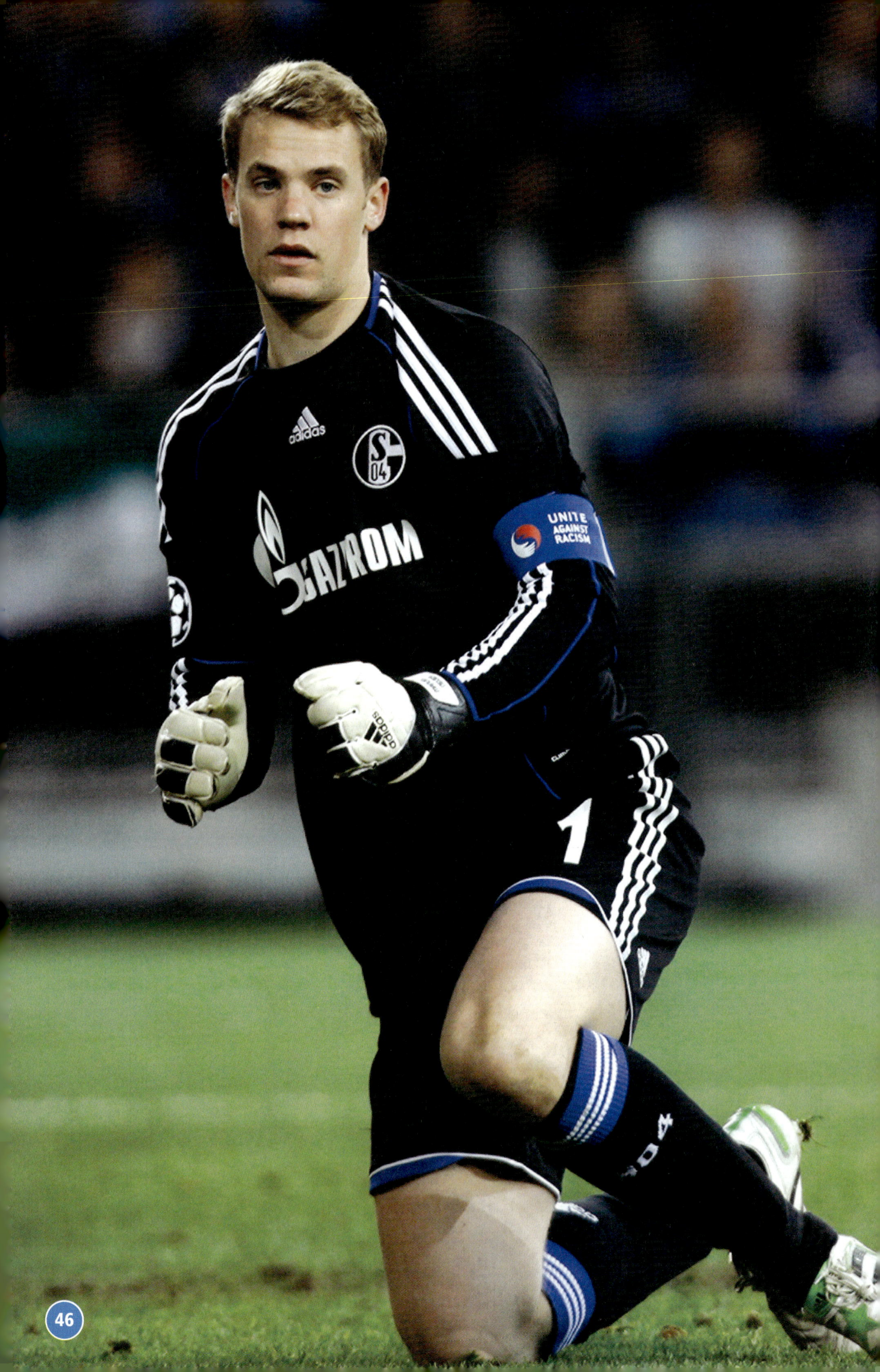

adidas
GAZPROM
UNITE
AGAINST
RACISM

FAST FACTS

Did You Know?

No team from London has ever won the Champions League or European Cup, although Chelsea and Arsenal have both been in the final. With Tottenham playing in the competition for the first time in 2010/11, the capital launched a three-pronged attack but again came up short.

Inter Milan's exit from the 2010/11 Champions League to FC Schalke in the quarter-finals still means that no club has retained the title since the format of the competition changed in 1992/3. AC Milan were the last team to mount a successful defence – winning the European Cup in 1989/90.

The first British club to take part in the European Cup was Hibernian. The Scottish club was invited to take part and reached the semi-finals of the inaugural competition in 1955-56. The Football League declined to enter English champions Chelsea.

In 2010/11, FC Copenhagen became the first Danish club to reach the knock-out stages of the Champions League. Their run was ended by Chelsea in the last 16.

Olympique Marseille set a new Champions League record when they beat Slovak side MSK Zilinia 7-0 in the group stages of the 2010/11 competition. It was the biggest away win in Champions League history.

Celtic were the first British team to win the European Cup. The 'Lisbon Lions' beat Inter Milan 2-1 in the final in Portugal in 1967.

From 1971 to 1981 only four clubs won the European Cup: Ajax (3), Bayern Munich (3), Liverpool (3) and Nottingham Forest (2). English clubs won it for six years in a row with Aston Villa (1982) following on from the dominance of Liverpool and Forest.

Ryan Giggs became the oldest player to score in the Champions League when he netted in the 2010/11 semi-finals against FC Schalke at the age of 37 years and 148 days. A new record had previously been set twice during the 2010/11 tournament by fellow 37-year-olds Javier Zanetti and Filippo Inzaghi.

RANGERS

Home Sweet Home for Walter

Walter Smith enjoyed a glorious finale to his second coming as manager of Rangers by securing a tenth Scottish Premier League title for the Ibrox club.

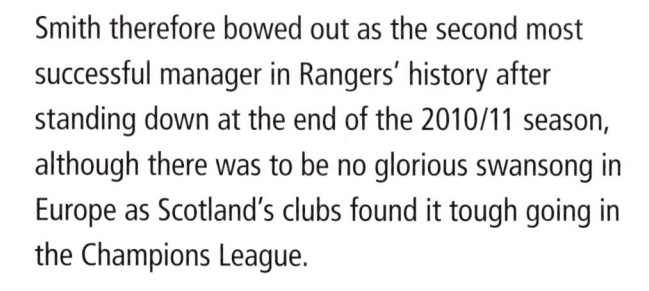

Smith therefore bowed out as the second most successful manager in Rangers' history after standing down at the end of the 2010/11 season, although there was to be no glorious swansong in Europe as Scotland's clubs found it tough going in the Champions League.

Celtic were unfortunate to be drawn against eventual Europa League runners-up SC Braga in their Champions League qualifier and after getting caught cold in their first game of the season lost 3-0 in Portugal.

That left Neil Lennon's side facing an uphill battle in the return leg and despite a 2-1 win, thanks to goals from Gary Hooper and Efrain Juarez, Celtic were left with too much to do and headed for the Europa League themselves.

As reigning SPL champions, Rangers kicked off in the group stage and made an encouraging start with a 0-0 draw at cross-border rivals Manchester United.

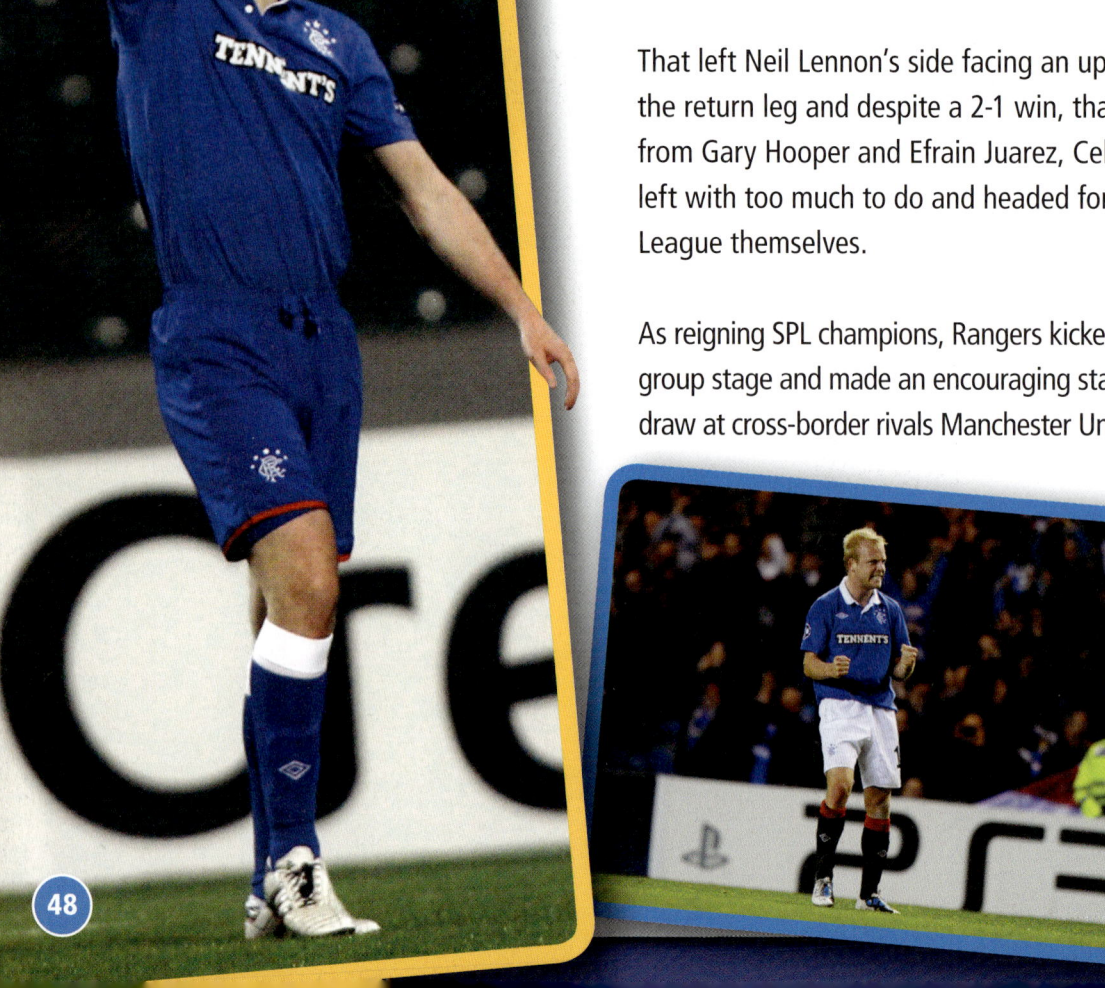

And when they followed that up with 1-0 win over Turkish side Bursaspor – their first victory in 13 European ties – thanks to a goal from Steven Naismith, the Gers sat proudly at the top of Group C alongside United.

A double-header next up against Valencia looked to be key to qualification and honours finished even at Ibrox Park with Rangers defender Mo Edu scoring at both ends.

But a 3-0 defeat in Spain edged Rangers out of the qualification spots and confirmation of their exit from the Champions League came via a late Wayne Rooney penalty in the re-match with United in Glasgow.

The Gers had booked a Europa League spot, though, as they finished third in the group with a Kenny Miller goal in Turkey giving them another draw from a 1-1 scoreline with Bursaspor.

Smith had delivered an extended bout of European competition and although there was to be no repeat of their run to the 2008 Europa League final, glory days still lay ahead for one last time for the Ibrox legend.

WORDSEARCH

F	I	A	R	S	E	N	A	L	X	I	Y	K	Y	F
L	M	B	S	T	V	G	V	A	E	U	R	O	P	A
E	E	T	E	X	Z	D	U	U	N	I	T	E	D	R
Y	K	I	W	P	I	O	N	A	O	E	D	M	Y	Z
E	L	D	W	M	E	S	S	I	R	I	N	P	V	M
L	A	A	L	O	N	P	O	F	R	D	R	T	J	V
B	H	S	E	F	O	Q	E	D	G	O	I	S	C	N
M	C	G	N	S	J	H	A	U	O	A	N	O	B	Q
E	S	M	I	L	L	M	Y	N	G	O	C	S	L	E
W	H	A	V	E	E	E	E	Y	I	A	E	N	J	A
Y	X	D	P	R	L	Y	H	P	B	J	E	D	C	S
C	T	R	O	P	H	Y	M	C	W	A	K	L	G	P
E	U	H	A	A	B	A	R	C	E	L	O	N	A	U
F	C	I	Q	R	H	B	R	Y	Y	U	M	C	N	R
M	D	L	R	C	G	S	G	V	X	G	V	D	M	S

Wembley **Guardiola** **Spurs**

Barcelona **Champions** **Chelsea**

United **League** **Arsenal**

Messi **Madrid** **Trophy**

Rooney **Schalke** **Europa**

Answers on page 61

50

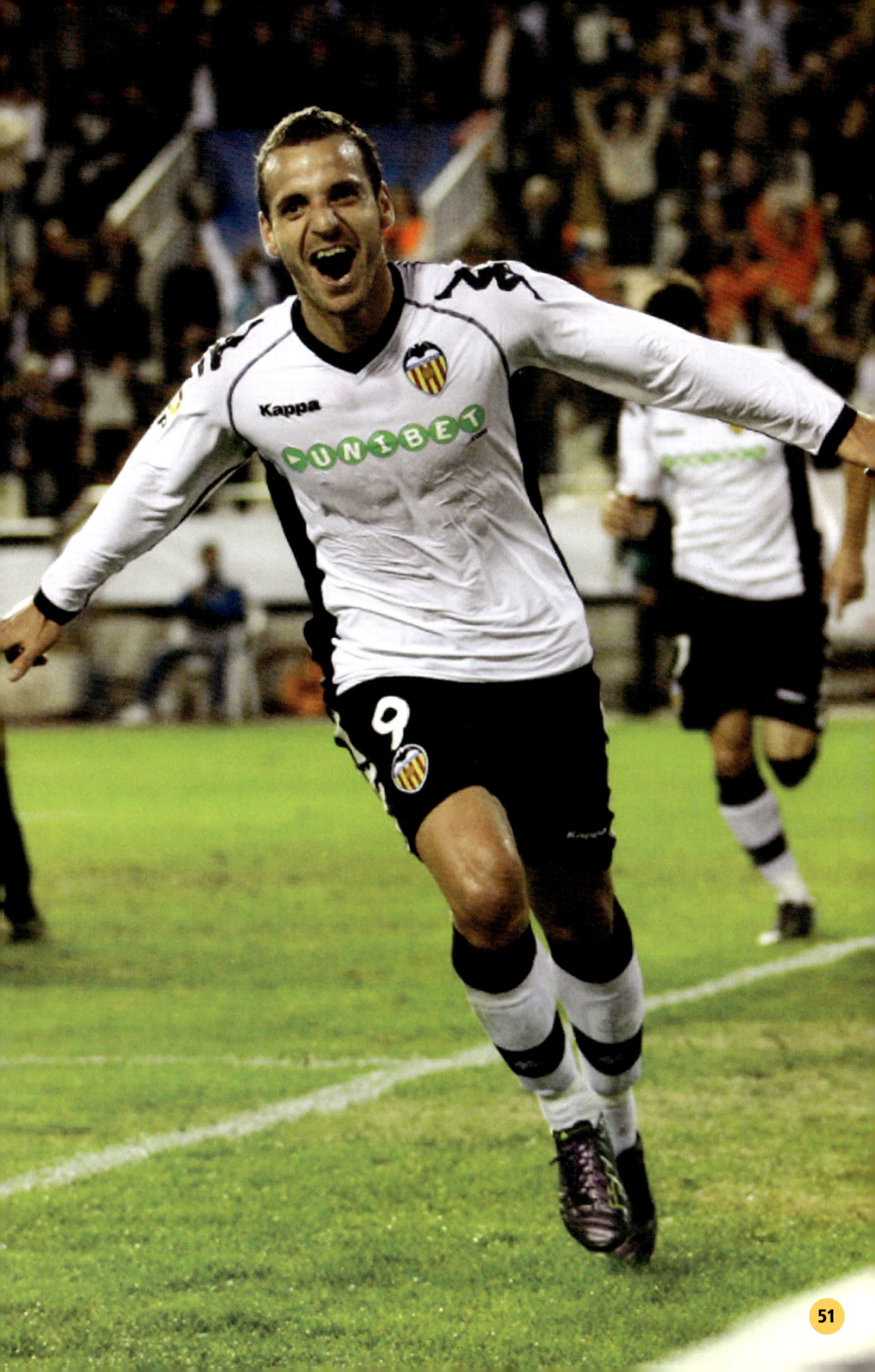
Kappa
UNIBET

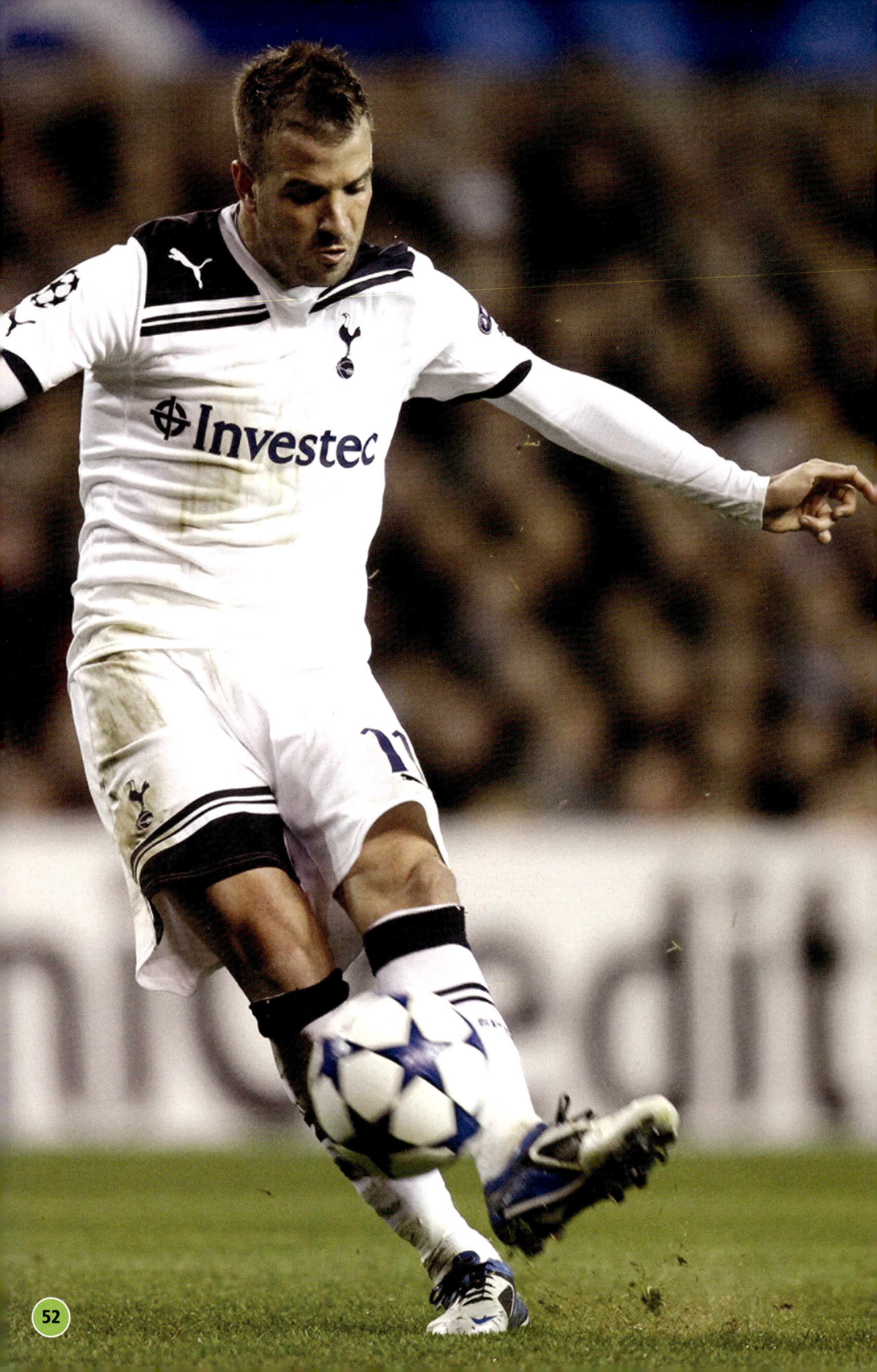
Investec

FUN AND GAMES

Answers on page 61

GOAL!
Un-scramble lines to find who scores the winning goal.

MAZE

ANAGRAM
Un-scramble the letters to find these former winners of the Champions League.

1. RLLPOOVIE
2. SJNTUVEU
3. RAYNEB NUHICM
4. TPOOR
5. ASRELMLIE
6. ARLE RDIMAD

53

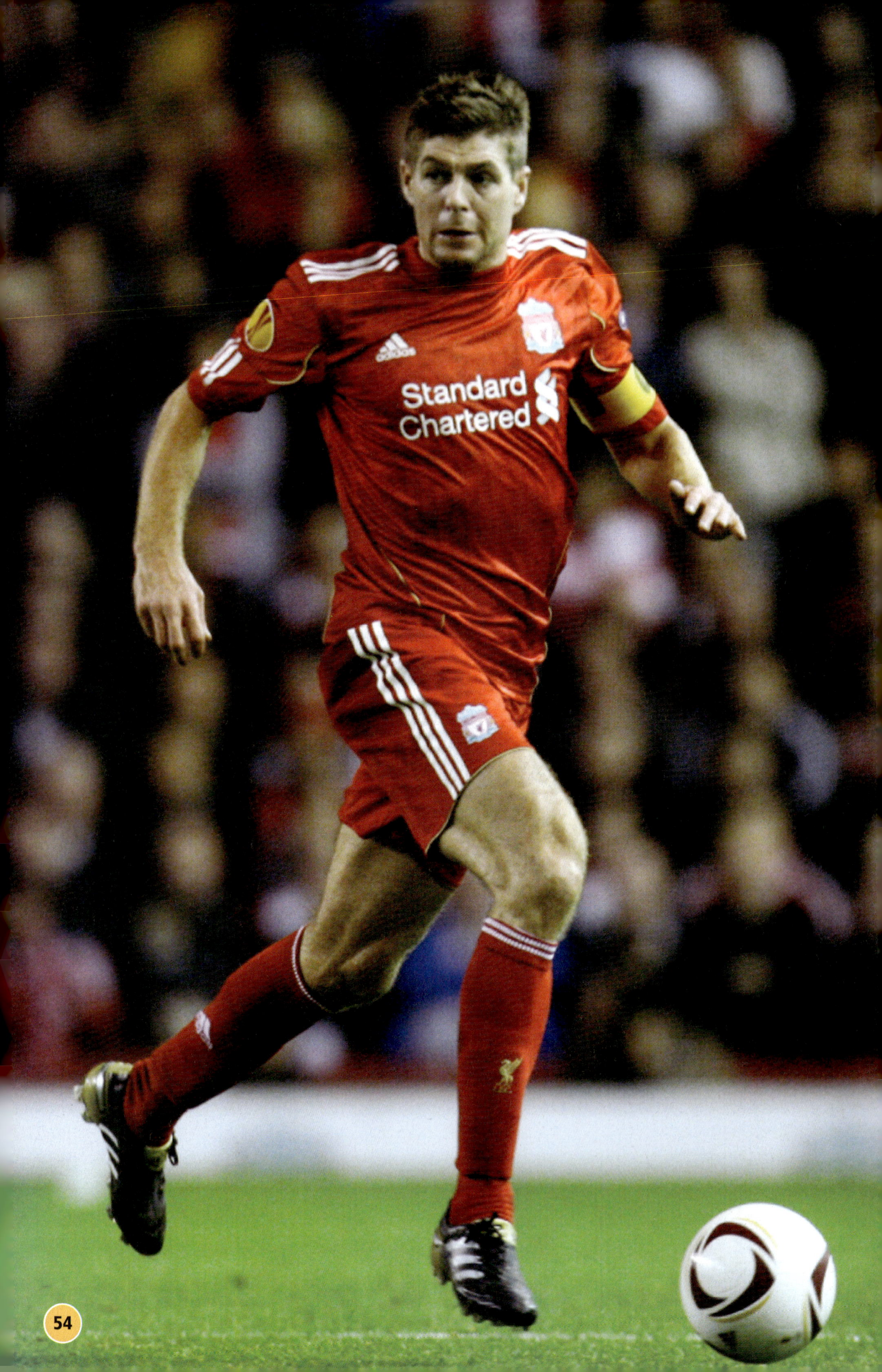
Standard Chartered

Back Home With Barca

Champions return in triumph

Just 24 hours after their thrilling final triumph success over Manchester United, Barcelona were back home to celebrate with their fans.

Around one million people packed the streets of Barcelona to see their heroes return with the Champions League trophy.

The Barca team kicked off at the city's World Trade Centre as they proudly displayed the silverware from their 21st Spanish La Liga title and their triumphant European campaign.

Pepe Guardiola and his team then paraded through the streets on an open-top bus before reaching their Nou Camp home.

There the players were presented individually to an ecstatic crowd before a final, well-deserved lap of honour.

"Thanks so much to you all for making us feel so happy," Guardiola added.

"Your support through the year has been great and we hope to repeat these feats next year."

The rest of Europe has been warned!

PORTUGUESE PRIDE

The Special One Mark II

Porto are pride of Portugal in Europa League

FC Porto got their name back on the European roll of honour thanks to a coach who could become the new Special One!

Porto's success in the Europa League gave them their first non-domestic silverware since Jose Mourinho led them to Champions League glory in 2004.

Mourinho has since gone on to add to his glittering CV at Chelsea, Inter Milan and Real Madrid.

And having guided Porto to a hat-trick of trophies, Andre Villas-Boas is following further in Mourinho's glittering footsteps by taking over as Chelsea's new manager.

Porto's 1-0 victory over SC Braga in the all-Portuguese Europa League final in Dublin – secured by Radamel Falcao's 17th goal of the tournament – made Villas-Boas the youngest coach to win a European club competition at the age of just 33.

After learning his trade as a coach under Sir Bobby Robson and then in Mourinho's backroom staff in Porto, London and Milan, Villas-Boas took his first senior post with Portuguese club Academica at the start of the 2009/10 season.

Twelve months later he joined Porto and was an instant hit by winning the treble of the Europa League and Portuguese league and cup in 2011.

With that on his CV, Chelsea made their move and secured one of the brightest young managers in the game on a three-year contract to replace Carlo Ancelotti at Stamford Bridge, making the Champions League – and a potential clash with Mourinho – Villas-Boas' next big target.

57

PORTUGUESE PRIDE

While Portugal were also represented in the semi-finals by Benfica, the 2010/11 Europa League wasn't a great success for England and Scotland.

North of the border, Hibernian went out in the third qualifying round, while Celtic, Dundee United and Motherwell failed to make it past the play-off stage.

Rangers dropped out of the Champions League but survived just one round before losing to PSV Eindhoven in the last 16.

English clubs fared no better with Aston Villa crashing out at the play-off stage with a shock home defeat to Rapid Vienna and Liverpool and Manchester City both falling at the last-16 hurdle.

Kenny Dalglish's return to Anfield had Reds' fans dreaming of more Euro glory but it didn't turn out to be a vintage campaign.

Under Roy Hodgson Liverpool advanced as unbeaten group winners with a second-half hat-trick via the bench from substitute Steven Gerrard against Lazio among the highlights.

But Europa League goals proved in short supply following the much heralded arrival of Dalglish for a second spell as manager.

It took a later header from Dirk Kuyt for the five-times champions of Europe to scrape past Sparta Prague in the first knock-out round.

But even with the introduction of record-buy Andy Carroll, Liverpool couldn't find an equalising goal at home to Braga in the second leg of their last-16 clash to prevent the Portugese side from advancing towards the final 1-0 on aggregate.

Big-spending City also topped their group and enjoyed a comfortable passage to the last 16 thanks to a 3-0 home win over Greek club Aris Thessaloniki as Edin Dzeko scored his first European goals for his new club.

But a 2-0 defeat away to Dynamo Kiev, with European legend Andriy Shevchenko getting one of the goals, left City's hopes of glory hanging by a thread.

There was to be no escape as City, down to ten men following Mario Balotelli's red card, could manage only an Aleksandar Kolarov goal in the return leg.

Roberto Mancini's men finished the season on a high, though, as they booked their place in the Champions League for the first time.

STAT ATTACK

Did You Know?

The attendance for the 2011 final at Wembley was 87,695 – the second-biggest crowd for a Champions League final. In 1999 Manchester United beat Bayern Munich in front of 90,045 at the Nou Camp.

An estimated television audience of over 300 million watched the final between Barcelona and Manchester United.

Taking into account prize money and money from the television marketing pool, Barcelona were expected to make around £50 million from their latest Champions League triumph.

The 2010/11 Champions League involved 125 matches from the group stages onwards.

According to statistics from Opta, Barcelona made 777 passes in the final, compared with United's 357. Of those, 148 came from Barca midfielder Xavi with a 95 per cent completion rate while goalkeeper Victor Valdes made 18 passes – two more than United striker Javier Hernandez.

Slovakian side MSK Zilina and Partizan Belgrade of Serbia both failed to collect a point in the group stages of the 2010/11 competition.

A total of 76 teams entered the 2011/12 Champions League. The first qualifying round kicked off on June 28.

North London rivals Spurs and Arsenal were top scorers in the group stage with 18 goals apiece. Manchester United boasted the meanest defence, conceding just once.

QUIZ ANSWERS

CHAMPIONS LEAGUE QUIZ

1. Pedro Rodriguez
2. Hungary
3. Manchester United
4. Gareth Bale
5. FC Copenhagen
6. Russia
7. Raul
8. Bayern Munich
9. Edwin van der Sar
10. Eric Abidal
11. Munich
12. Manchester City

GOAL! SOLUTION

Wayne Rooney

ANAGRAM SOLUTIONS

1. Liverpool
2. Juventus
3. Bayern Munich
4. Porto
5. Marseille
6. Real Madrid

WORDSEARCH SOLUTION

MAZE SOLUTION

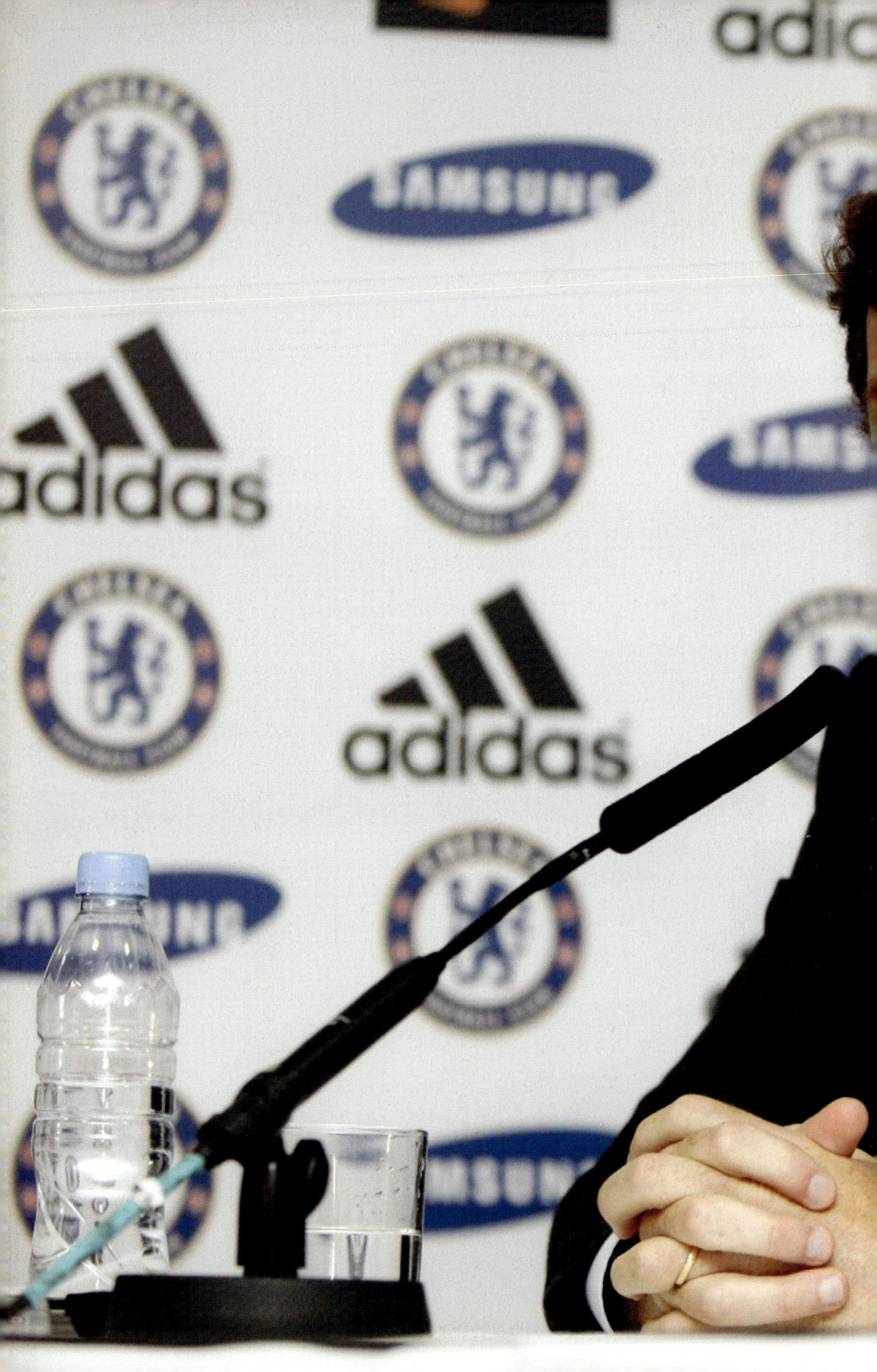
adidas
adidas